GEARING UP FOR SPORTS!



# SOCCER GEAR

NOAH RICCARDI

PowerKiDS press™

Published in 2027 by The Rosen Publishing Group, Inc.
2544 Clinton Street, Buffalo, NY 14224



First Edition

Book Design: Madison Thogmartin

Photo Credits: Cover, p. 1 Fotokostic/Shutterstock.com; p. 5 matimix/Shutterstock.com; p. 7 Nattawit Khomsanit/Shutterstock.com; p. 9 Raffaele Conti 88/Shutterstock.com; p. 11 Ringo Chiu/Shutterstock.com; p. 13 Le Do/Shutterstock.com; p. 15 IOIO Images/Shutterstock.com; p. 17 Jose Breton- Pics Action/Shutterstock.com; p. 19 Vlad1988/Shutterstock.com; p. 21 Fabrizio Andrea Bertani/Shutterstock.com.

Cataloging-in-Publication Data
Names: Riccardi, Noah.
Title: Soccer gear / Noah Riccardi.
Description: Buffalo, New York : PowerKids Press, 2027. | Series: Gearing up for sports! | Includes glossary and index.
Identifiers: ISBN 9781499456738 (pbk.) | ISBN 9781499456745 (library bound) | ISBN 9781499456752 (ebook)
Subjects: LCSH: Soccer--Juvenile literature. | Soccer--Equipment and supplies--Juvenile literature.
Classification: LCC GV943.9 R533 2027 | DDC 796.334--dc23

Manufactured in China

CPSIA Compliance Information: Batch #QS27PK. For Further Information contact Rosen Publishing, at 1-800-237-9932.

# CONTENTS

# The Ball

Soccer players try to kick a ball into a goal. The ball is round and **inflated** with air. The outside of the ball is made from a firm material.

9
11

Soccer balls come in different sizes. Young players play with size three balls. Pro leagues use size five. Size three balls are about 7.5 inches (19 cm) across. Size five balls are about 8.75 inches (22.2 cm) wide.

adidas
AL RIHLA
OFFICIAL MATCH BALL
FIFA WORLD CUP
Qatar2022
SPEEDSHELL

# Boots

Soccer players wear shoes with spikes on the bottom. These shoes are called boots. They are sometimes called cleats. The spikes grip the ground. This stops players from slipping. Players may use longer spikes in the rain.

Players can kick the ball with many parts of the boot. Players **shoot** the ball using the top of the foot, or the laces. They **pass** the ball using the inside of the foot.

Emirates
FLY BETTER
AFC
AFC

## Shin Guards

Soccer players might kick or run into each other. Players wear shin guards to protect their lower legs. Players slide shin guards into long socks. Some shin guards are also attached to smaller pads that protect the ankles.

## Socks

Soccer players wear long socks. The socks go up to the knee. This protects players' legs from getting scratched by grass or **turf**. These socks also help hold shin guards in place.

20
AUS

## Soccer Kits

Players wear uniforms called kits. Teams' kits have different colors. This helps tell teams apart. The shirts have numbers and names on the back. This helps people tell players apart.

21
USA
4

Kit colors can become important to teams. These colors can be part of a team's **culture**. Fans can wear kits, too. Wearing a kit is a common way for people to support their team.

# Goalkeeper Gloves

**Goalkeepers** defend their team's goal. They can touch the ball with their hands. To protect their hands, goalkeepers wear padded gloves. Some gloves have **rigid** fingers. This stops the goalkeeper's fingers from bending backwards.

# GLOSSARY

**culture:** The ideas and traditions of a group.

**goalkeepers:** Soccer players who may use their hands to defend the goal.

**inflated:** Filled with air or some other gas.

**pass:** To kick the ball to a teammate.

**rigid:** Hard to bend.

**shoot:** To kick the ball at the goal.

**turf:** Fake grass made from plastic and rubber.

# FOR MORE INFORMATION

## BOOKS

Leatherland, Noah. *Soccer*. Mendota Heights, MN: North Star Editions, 2026.

Wagner, Zelda. *Soccer Superstars*. Minneapolis, MN: Lerner Publications, 2025.

## WEBSITES

**Britannica Kids: World Cup**
*kids.britannica.com/kids/article/World-Cup/390872*
Find out about soccer's biggest competition.

**Olympics: Football (soccer)**
*olympics.com/en/sports/football/*
Learn about soccer at the Olympic Games.

Publisher's note to educators and parents: Our editors have carefully reviewed these websites to ensure that they are suitable for students. Many websites change frequently, however, and we cannot guarantee that a site's future contents will continue to meet our high standards of quality and educational value. Be advised that students should be closely supervised whenever they access the internet.

# INDEX